660 feet
(200 meters)

WEIRD-BUT-TRUE FACTS ABOUT SCIENCE

BY ARNOLD RINGSTAD • ILLUSTRATED BY KATHLEEN PETELINSEK

Published by The Child's World®
1980 Lookout Drive • Mankato, MN 56003-1705
800-599-READ • www.childsworld.com

Acknowledgments
The Child's World®: Mary Berendes, Publishing Director
Red Line Editorial: Editorial direction
The Design Lab: Design
Amnet: Production

ISBN 9781614734178
LCCN 2012946524

Printed in the United States of America
Mankato, MN
November, 2012
PA02143

About the Author

Arnold Ringstad lives in Minneapolis,
Minnesota. He enjoys building and
launching rockets, even if they aren't
36 stories tall.

About the Illustrator

Kathleen Petelinsek loves to draw and
paint. She lives next to a lake in southern
Minnesota with her husband, Dale; two
daughters, Leah and Anna; two dogs,
Gary and Rex; and her fluffy cat, Emma.

TABLE OF CONTENTS

INTRODUCTION

Scientists have been making discoveries about our universe for thousands of years. They study the stars in the sky and the center of the sun. They investigate the extremely hot and the extremely cold, the gigantic and the tiny. They seek patterns in numbers and mathematics. They even discover how time and space interact. Scientists have learned much about how the universe works. Get ready to learn about some fascinating discoveries and the interesting people who made them. And don't forget—these facts are all true!

SPACE AND PLANET STATS

There are more stars in the universe than there are grains of sand on all of Earth's beaches.

One teaspoon of a neutron star weighs more than 100 million tons (90 million metric tons).

A neutron star is a very small, very dense star that is made when a large star collapses. Neutron stars have a lot of tightly packed **mass**.

1 teaspoon

100 MILLION TONS

If Earth were the size of a golf ball, the sun would be 15 feet (4.5 m) wide.

But even the sun is tiny compared to other stars. On this scale, one of the largest stars in the galaxy would be the size of Mount Everest.

The winds on Neptune are more than five times faster than the strongest wind ever recorded on Earth.

They are the strongest in the solar system. Winds on Neptune blow at 1,500 miles per hour (2,400 km/h).

15 feet

The temperature on the surface of Venus can reach nearly 900 degrees Fahrenheit (482°C).

This is about seven times hotter than the hottest temperatures on Earth. It's also hotter than most ovens.

The planet Jupiter has more mass than the rest of the planets put together.

There are less than two Mercury days in a Mercury year.

A year on Mercury—the time it takes to rotate the sun—is only 88 Earth days. But a Mercury day—the time it takes to spin on its axis—is more than 58 Earth days.

Energy takes about one million years to get from the center of the sun to the surface of the sun.

The energy travels about 430,000 miles (692,000 km) through very hot burning gases. At the surface, the energy is released as light. The light then takes only eight minutes to travel 93 million miles (150 million km) from the surface of the sun to Earth.

For the Northern Hemisphere, Earth is closer to the sun during winter than it is during summer.

When Earth is tilted so that the sun's light is hitting it more directly, it heats up and causes summer, even though the sun is farther away.

Until 2006, there were nine planets in the solar system.

In that year, scientists decided to call Pluto a dwarf planet instead. Now there are eight planets.

There is a giant meteor crater in the desert in Arizona.

Barringer Crater is about 4,000 feet (1,200 m) across and 650 feet (200 m) deep. It was created 50,000 years ago when a meteor more than 100 feet (30 m) wide smashed into the ground.

660 feet
(200 meters)

Sunlight can reach about 660 feet (200 m) down into the ocean.

The deepest part of the ocean is about 36,000 feet (11,000 m).

Mars' moon Phobos has such low gravity that you could easily throw a baseball into orbit from its surface.

It is only about 12 miles (20 km across).

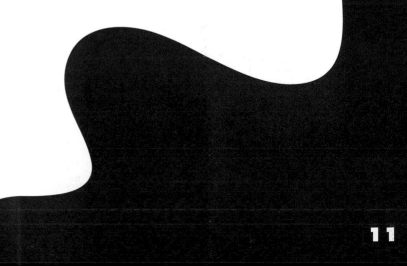

ELEMENT EXTREMES

You can melt the metal gallium by holding it in your hand.

Its melting point is about 86 degrees Fahrenheit (30°C). The melting point of carbon is about 6,870 degrees Fahrenheit (3,800°C). The melting point of water, when it goes from a solid to a liquid, is 32 degrees Fahrenheit (0°C).

We could be up to our knees in gold.

There is enough gold hidden in the planet's crust that it could cover Earth's landmasses to about the depth of someone's knees.

One ounce (0.03 kg) of gold can be flattened into a thin sheet covering about 270 square feet (25 sq m).

This is 400 times thinner than a human hair.

If you pour salt into a full glass of water, the glass won't overflow.

The water level will actually go down. This is because the salt **molecules** fill into the space between the water molecules.

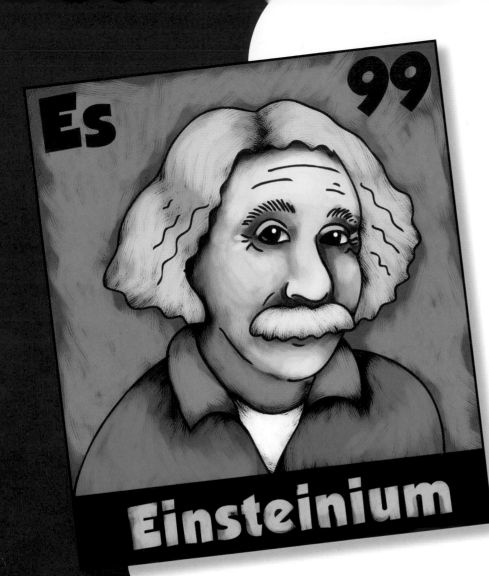

Es 99

Einsteinium

Several elements are named after people or places.

These include Einsteinium (after Albert Einstein), Californium (after the state of California), and Mendelevium (after Dmitri Mendeleev, the creator of the periodic table of elements).

There is about 1/2 pound (0.2 kg) of salt in the average human body.

Some metal elements explode or start fires when dropped in water.

These include cesium, rubidium, and potassium.

There is only about 1 ounce (28 g) of the element astatine on Earth.

This makes it the rarest element in the world. It occurs naturally in Earth's crust, but it doesn't last long, so at any given time very little exists. Scientists have also created it in laboratories.

PHYSICS FACTS

Bullets hit the ground at the same time whether they're shot from a gun or dropped.

If you shoot a bullet straight forward at the same time you drop a bullet from the same height, both will hit the ground at the same time. But, the bullet you dropped will be at your feet and the bullet you shot will be hundreds of feet away. This is because gravity works on the two bullets at the same rate, no matter how fast the bullet travels.

Sound travels at about 750 mph (1,200 km/h) through air.

It goes about four times faster through water, and ten times faster through glass.

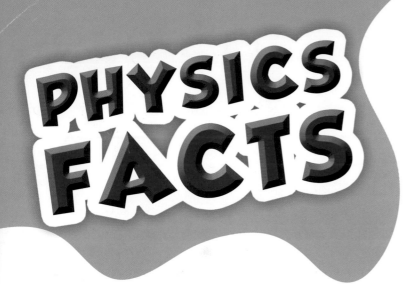

If there was a hole that led to the center of Earth and you dropped a ball down it, it would take about 42 minutes to get to the other side of the planet.

You need to throw a ball twice as hard to pitch it 100 mph (160 km/h) than you do to pitch it 70 mph (113 km/h).

It is impossible to go faster than the speed of light.

Light travels at about 186,000 miles per second (300,000,000 km/s). It takes light from the moon takes less than two seconds to reach Earth.

When people go into space, they are about 2 inches (5 cm) taller than they are on Earth.

This is because gravity is not pushing down on them.

The faster you move, the heavier you get.

The difference is only noticeable at very high speeds, close to the speed of light.

You weigh about six times more on Earth than you would on the moon.

This is because the moon has weaker gravity.

ASTRONAUTS' ADVENTURES

The astronauts on Apollo 10 traveled at almost 25,000 miles per hour (40,000 km/h).

They set the speed record for human beings as they came back to Earth in 1968.

There are about 3,000 man-made satellites orbiting the Earth.

The first one was launched in 1957.

The record for time spent in space by a person is 803 days.

The record was set by Sergei Krikalev, a Russian **cosmonaut**.

The Saturn V moon rocket stood 363 feet (110.6 m) tall.

This is as tall as a 36-story building. It launched U.S. astronauts to the first moon landing in 1969. As of 2012, it was still the tallest and heaviest rocket ever launched.

U.S. astronauts brought back 842 pounds (382 kg) of rocks and soil from the moon.

They made six landings between 1969 and 1972. Some of these rocks can be found at the National Air and Space Museum at the Smithsonian Institute in Washington, DC.

NUMBER NEWS

If there are 23 people in the room, there is a 50 percent chance that two of them share the same birthday.

Four is the only number that has the same number of letters as its spelling.

If you spell out the numbers starting at zero, the letter "a" doesn't appear until you reach one thousand.

A "googol" is the number 1 with 100 zeroes after it.

A "googolplex" is an even bigger number that is a 1 with a googol of zeroes after it. There is not enough room in the universe to write the numbers from one to a googolplex, no matter how small you write them.

You can find a mathematical pattern in seashells, animal horns, and sunflowers.

The pattern, Fibonacci's sequence, begins 1, 1, 2, 3, 5, 8, 13, 21. Each number in the pattern is found by adding together the two previous numbers (2=1 + 1; 3 = 2 + 1; 8 = 5 + 3, and so on). Spirals in nature grow according to this pattern.

ABCDE**F**GHIJKLMN**O**PQ**R**S**T**UVWX**Y**z

It would take about 12 days to count to 1 million at one number per second.

It would take about 32 years to count to 1 billion, and more than 31,000 years to count to 1 trillion.

The only number whose letters are in alphabetical order is 40.

One is the only number whose letters are in reverse alphabetical order.

THE ODD LIVES OF SCIENTISTS

Astronomer William Herschel wanted to name the planet he discovered "the Georgian Planet" after King George III.

It was later renamed "Uranus" after the ancient Greek god of the sky.

Astronomer Tycho Brahe had a piece of his nose made of silver and gold.

He lost part of it in a fight and created his own replacement. Brahe lived in the 1500s and made detailed records about the movements of the stars and planets.

The Greek scientist Eratosthenes was the first person to figure out the size of Earth, more than 2,000 years ago.

He used the angle of the sun in the sky to calculate it.

Isaac Newton tried but failed to turn common metals into gold.

This is known as **alchemy**. He had to do it secretly because it was illegal at the time.

The scientist and inventor Nikola Tesla claimed to receive radio signals from the planet Mars in 1899.

Albert Einstein began studying calculus at age 12.

At school, he excelled in math and science and also played the violin. However, he was so bad at French he failed his university entrance exam the first time he took it.

Charles Darwin ate an owl, a hawk, a puma, and a Galapagos tortoise.

At Cambridge University, he was a member of the Gourmet Club. Club members got together to eat animals not usually served for dinner, including hawk and owl. He continued his unusual eating habits on the voyage of the ship *Beagle* to the Pacific Ocean. On that trip, he sampled puma, Galapagos tortoise, armadillo, and an ostrich-like bird called the rhea.

GLOSSARY

alchemy (AL-kuh-mee)
Alchemy is the process of transforming common metals into gold. Isaac Newton had to practice alchemy in secret.

calculus (KAL-kyuh-lus)
Calculus is an advanced branch of mathematics. Albert Einstein studied calculus at a young age.

element (EL-uh-munt)
An element is a substance that can't be broken into other things. Gold is an element.

gravity (GRAV-uh-tee)
Gravity is the force that pulls things toward stars, planets, and other bodies.

The Earth has stronger gravity than the moon.

mass (MASS)
Mass is the amount of material inside something. Jupiter has much more mass than the rest of the planets.

molecules (MALL-uh-kyul)
Molecules are the smallest parts of a substance. Salt molecules can fit into the spaces between water molecules.

neutron star (NOO-tron STAR)
A neutron star is a dense body in space created from the collapse of a larger star. A neutron star has a lot of mass for its size.

LEARN MORE

BOOKS

Space Facts: DK Pockets.
New York: DK Publishing,
2003.

*TIME for Kids BIG Book of
Why: 1,001 Facts Kids Want
to Know.* New York: TIME
for Kids, 2010.

WEB SITES

Visit our Web site for links
about weird science facts:
childsworld.com/links

*Note to Parents, Teachers, and
Librarians: We routinely verify our
Web links to make sure they are safe
and active sites. So encourage your
readers to check them out!*

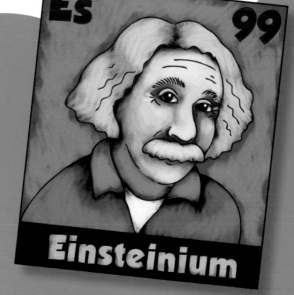

Es 99
Einsteinium

INDEX